SONGS FROM
HEAVEN AND EARTH

Selections from the Psalms

Published in Nashville, Tennessee, by Thomas Nelson, Inc. and distributed in
Canada by Lawson Falle, Ltd., Cambridge, Ontario.

The Scriptures in this book are from the New King James Version. Copyright ©
1979, 1980, 1982, Thomas Nelson, Inc., Publishers.

Text selections followed by the initials JB are by Jill Briscoe.
Text selections followed by the initials SB are by Stuart Briscoe.

Printed in Singapore by Tien Wah Press (pte.) Ltd.

ISBN 0-8407-4151-0

SONGS FROM
HEAVEN AND EARTH

Selections from the Psalms in the New King James Version

Text by Jill and Stuart Briscoe

Thomas Nelson Publishers
Nashville • Camden • New York

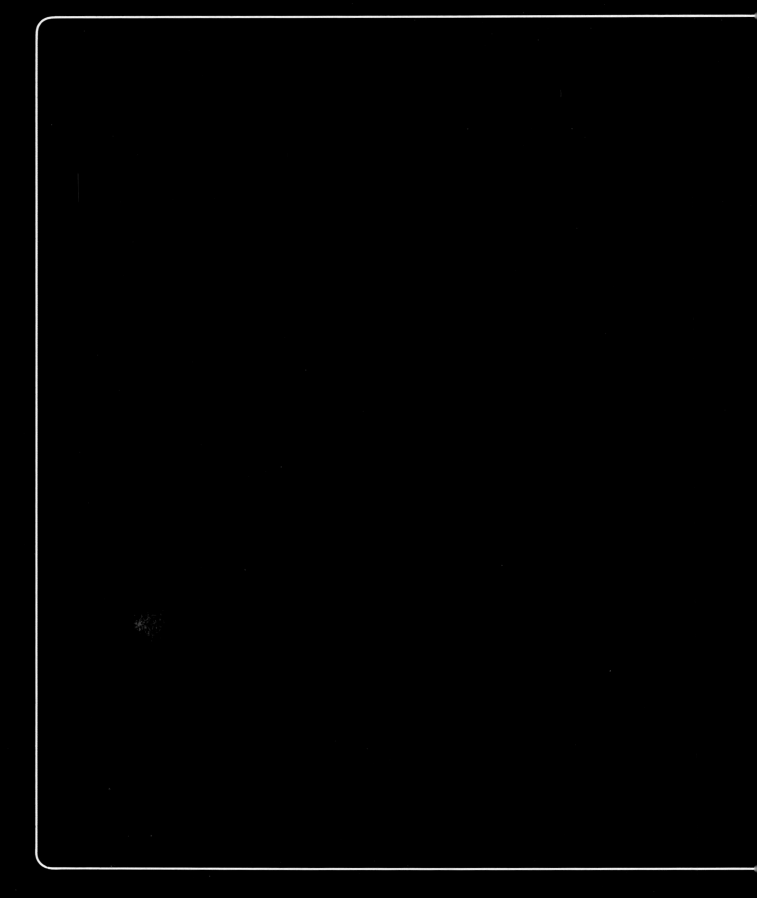

Let the heavens rejoice,
and let the earth be glad;
let the sea roar,
and all its
fullness.

Before the mountains
were brought forth,
or ever You had formed
the earth and the world,
even from everlasting
to everlasting
You are God.

All My Fountains Are in You

His foundation is in the holy mountains.
This LORD loves the gates of Zion
more than all the dwellings of Jacob.
Glorious things are spoken of you,
O city of God!   Selah
"I will make mention of Rahab and
Babylon to those who know Me;
behold, O Philistia and Tyre,
with Ethiopia:
'This one was born there.'
And of Zion it will be said,
"This one and that one were born in her;
and the Most High Himself shall
establish her."
The LORD will record,
when He registers the peoples:
"This one was born there."   Selah
Both the singers and the players on
instruments say,
"All my springs are in you."

*It is so good to know where You
stand, Lord. Your commitments have
been made and You have made them
known. You have also let me know
where I stand in relation to You. My
sense of security is superb. Truly my
resources are in You.—SB*

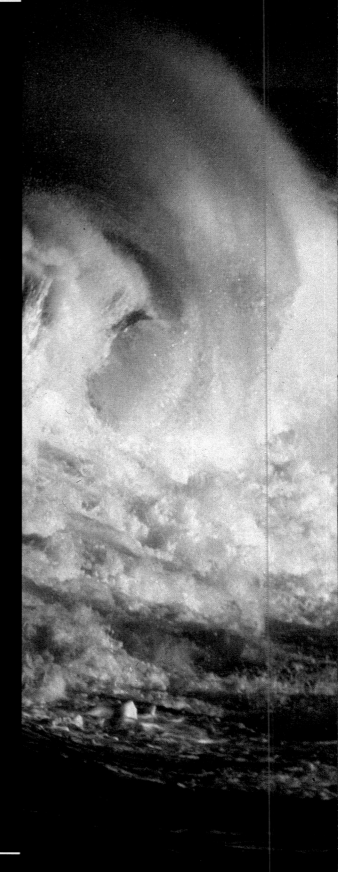

I Cry before You

O LORD, God of my salvation,
I have cried out day and night before You.
Let my prayer come before You;
incline Your ear to my cry.
For my soul is full of troubles,
and my life draws near to the grave.
I am counted with those who go down to the pit;
I am like a man who has no strength,
adrift among the dead,
like the slain who lie in the grave,
whom You remember no more,
and who are cut off from Your hand.
You have laid me in the lowest pit,
in darkness, in the depths.
Your wrath lies heavy upon me,
and You have afflicted me with all Your waves.   Selah
You have put away my acquaintances far from me;
You have made me an abomination to them;
I am shut up, and I cannot get out;
my eye wastes away because of affliction.
LORD, I have called daily upon You;
I have stretched out my hands to You.
Will You work wonders for the dead?
Shall the dead arise and praise You?   Selah
Shall Your lovingkindness be declared in the grave?
Or Your faithfulness in the place of destruction?
Shall Your wonders be known in the dark?
And Your righteousness in the land of forgetfulness?
But to You I have cried out, O LORD,
and in the morning my prayer comes before You.
LORD, why do You cast off my soul?
Why do You hide Your face from me?
I have been afflicted and ready to die
from my youth up;
I suffer Your terrors; I am distraught.
Your fierce wrath has gone over me;
Your terrors have cut me off.
They came around me all day long like water;
they engulfed me altogether.
Loved one and friend You have put far from me,
and my acquaintances into darkness.

*Drowning men snatch at straws. I feel I'm
sinking but straws won't help. So, Lord, I call
on You. I trust You but I don't always
understand. Your wrath is merited but can it
not be stayed? I honor You but I don't always
agree—so, Lord, see my sinking state and
deliver me from the darkness.—SB*

O Lord Almighty, Who Is like You?

I will sing of the mercies of the LORD forever;
with my mouth will I make known
Your faithfulness to all generations.
For I have said,
"Mercy shall be built up forever;
Your faithfulness You shall establish
in the very heavens."
"I have made a covenant with My chosen,
I have sworn to My servant David:
'Your seed I will establish forever,
and build up your throne to all generations.' "   Selah
And the heavens will praise Your wonders, O LORD;
Your faithfulness also in the congregation of the saints.
For who in the heavens can be compared to the LORD?
Who among the sons of the mighty can be likened
to the LORD?...
O LORD God of hosts,
who is mighty like You, O LORD?
Your faithfulness also surrounds You.
You rule the raging of the sea;
when its waves rise, You still them.
You have broken Rahab in pieces, as one who is slain;
You have scattered Your enemies with Your mighty arm.
The heavens are Yours, the earth also is Yours;
The world and all its fullness, You have founded them.
The north and the south, You have created them;
Tabor and Hermon rejoice in Your name.
You have a mighty arm; strong is Your hand,
and high is Your right hand.
Righteousness and justice are the foundation
of Your throne;
mercy and truth go before Your face.
Blessed are the people who know the joyful sound!
They walk, O LORD, in the light of Your countenance.
In Your name they rejoice all day long,
and in Your righteousness they are exalted.
For You are the glory of their strength,
and in Your favor our horn is exalted.
For our shield belongs to the LORD,
and our king to the Holy One of Israel.

"O Lord Almighty, Who Is like You?" The heavens know and the earth agrees that God's faithfulness is—surer than the ageless mountain, deeper than the bottomless ocean, sweeter than the praise of angels! I add my voice to their song; my generation needs to know!—SB

He Will Maintain His Kindness Forever

Then You spoke in a vision to
Your holy one, and said:
"I have given help to one who is mighty;
I have exalted one chosen from the
people....
The enemy shall not outwit him,
nor the son of wickedness afflict him.
I will beat down his foes before his face,
and plague those who hate him....
Also I will set his hand over the sea,
and his right hand over the rivers,
he shall cry to Me,
'You are my Father, my God,
and the rock of my salvation.'
Also I will make him My firstborn,
the highest of the kings of the earth.
My mercy I will keep for him forever,
and My covenant shall stand firm
with him.
His seed also I will make to endure forever,
and his throne as the days of heaven.
If his sons forsake My law
and do not walk in My judgments,
if they break My statutes
and do not keep My commandments,
then I will visit their transgression
with the rod,
and their iniquity with stripes.
Nevertheless My lovingkindness I will
not utterly take from him,
nor allow My faithfulness to fail.
My covenant I will not break,
nor alter the word that has gone
out of My lips.
Once I have sworn by My holiness;
I will not lie to David:
His seed shall endure forever,
and his throne as the sun before Me;
it shall be established forever
like the moon,
even like the faithful witness
in the sky."   Selah

*Even chosen servants need God's
sustenance and strength. God warns
us of enemies and weaknesses, of
children who will break their parents'
hearts. Being chosen is not easy, but
it means being safe forever!—JB*

God Hides Himself;
But Not Forever

But You have cast off and abhorred,
You have been furious with Your anointed.
You have renounced the covenant of Your servant;
You have profaned his crown by casting it to the ground.
You have broken down all his hedges;
You have brought his strongholds to ruin.
All who pass by the way plunder him;
He is a reproach to his neighbors.
You have exalted the right hand of his adversaries;
You have made all his enemies rejoice.
You have also turned back the edge of his sword,
and have not sustained him in the battle.
You have made his glory cease,
and cast his throne down to the ground.
The days of his youth You have shortened;
You have covered him with shame.   Selah
How long, LORD?
Will You hide Yourself forever?
Will Your wrath burn like fire?
Remember how short my time is;
for what futility have You created all the
children of men?
What man can live and not see death?
Can he deliver his life from the power
of the grave?   Selah
LORD, where are Your former lovingkindnesses,
which You swore to David in Your truth?
Remember, Lord, the reproach of Your servants—
how I bear in my bosom the reproach
of all the many peoples,
with which Your enemies have reproached, O LORD,
with which they have reproached the footsteps
of Your anointed.
Blessed be the LORD forevermore!
Amen and Amen.

The desert is desolate but not without grandeur.
To feel deserted by You is total desolation but
not hopelessness. There's a rightness about Your
putting distance between my sinfulness and
Your holiness. But don't forget me, Lord.—SB

Give Me a Heart of Wisdom

LORD, You have been our dwelling place
in all generations.
Before the mountains were brought forth,
or ever You had formed the earth and the world,
even from everlasting to everlasting,
You are God.
You turn man to destruction,
and say, "Return, O children of men."
For a thousand years in Your sight
are like yesterday when it is past,
and like a watch in the night.
You carry them away like a flood;
they are like a sleep.
In the morning they are like grass which grows up:
in the morning it flourishes and grows up;
in the evening it is cut down and withers....
For all our days have passed away in Your wrath;
we finish our years like a sigh.
The days of our lives are seventy years;
and if by reason of strength they are eighty years,
yet their boast is only labor and sorrow;
for it is soon cut off, and we fly away.
Who knows the power of Your anger?
For as the fear of You, so is Your wrath.
So teach us to number our days,
that we may gain a heart of wisdom.
Return, O LORD!
How long?
And have compassion on Your servants.
Oh, satisfy us early with Your mercy,
that we may rejoice and be glad all our days!
Make us glad according to the days in
which You have afflicted us,
and the years in which we have seen evil.
Let Your work appear to Your servants,
and Your glory to their children.
And let the beauty of the LORD our
God be upon us,
and establish the work of our hands for us;
yes, establish the work of our hands.

Teach me the lesson of the mountain, Lord. It is only immense; You are infinite. Teach me the lesson of the snow, Lord. It melts and flows in the sun—I will pass away, too. Teach me the lesson of the cloud, Lord. It reflects the glory of the sun and swirls in patterns of beauty—then like me, it drifts away. Teach me to number my days.—SB

The Lord Will Be My Dwelling

He who dwells in the secret place
of the Most High
shall abide under the shadow of the Almighty.
I will say of the LORD, "He is my refuge and my
fortress; my God, in Him I will trust."
Surely He shall deliver you from the
snare of the fowler
and from the perilous pestilence.
He shall cover you with His feathers,
and under His wings you shall take refuge;
His truth shall be your shield and buckler.
You shall not be afraid of the terror by night,
nor of the arrow that flies by day,
nor of the pestilence that walks in darkness,
nor of the destruction that lays waste at noonday.
A thousand may fall at your side,
and ten thousand at your right hand;
but it shall not come near you....
Because you have made the LORD,
who is my refuge,
even the Most High, your habitation,
no evil shall befall you,
nor shall any plague come near your dwelling;
for He shall give His angels charge over you,
to keep you in all your ways.
They shall bear you up in their hands,
lest you dash your foot against a stone.
You shall tread upon the lion and the cobra,
the young lion and the serpent
you shall trample under foot.
Because he has set his love upon Me,
therefore I will deliver him;
I will set him on high,
because he has known My name.
He shall call upon Me,
and I will answer him;
I will be with him in trouble;
I will deliver him and honor him.
With long life I will satisfy him,
and show him My salvation.

Shadows can be scarey. They can stop you from sleeping. But there is one shadow that is different. It is like the shadow a mother hen makes with her wing to hide her frightened chick. It is called the Almighty Shadow and it is big enough to shelter the whole, wide world!—JB

Both the singers
and the players
on instruments say,
"All my springs
are in you."

Planted in the House of the Lord

It is good to give thanks to the LORD,
and to sing praises to Your name,
O Most High;
to declare Your lovingkindness
in the morning,
and Your faithfulness every night, . . .
For You, LORD, have made me glad
through Your work;
I will triumph in the works of Your hands.
O LORD, how great are Your works!
Your thoughts are very deep.
A senseless man does not know,
nor does a fool understand this.
When the wicked spring up like grass,
and when all the workers
of iniquity flourish,
it is that they may be destroyed forever.
But You, LORD, are on high forevermore.
For behold, Your enemies, O LORD,
for behold, Your enemies shall perish;
all the workers of iniquity shall be
scattered.
But my horn You have exalted
like a wild ox;
I have been anointed with fresh oil.
My eye also has seen my desire
on my enemies;
my ears hear my desire on the wicked
who rise up against me.
The righteous shall flouish
like a palm tree,
he shall grow like a cedar in Lebanon.
Those who are planted in the house
of the LORD
shall flourish in the courts of our God.
They shall still bear fruit in old age;
they shall be fresh and flourishing,
to declare that the LORD is upright;
He is my rock, and there is no
unrighteousness in Him.

*Palm trees usually do not stay fresh
and green when they are old—unless
God plants them in His courts. Ask
Him to plant you in His house while
you are young, to keep you fresh and
flourishing all your days. A tree
planted by the Lord will always bear
fruit—He promised.—JB*

The Lord Reigns

The LORD reigns,
He is clothed with majesty;
the LORD is clothed,
He has girded Himself with strength.
Surely the world is established,
so that it cannot be moved.
Your throne is established from of old;
You are from everlasting.
The floods have lifted up, O LORD,
the floods have lifted up their voice;
the floods lift up their waves.
The LORD on high is mightier
than the noise of many waters,
than the mighty waves of the sea.
Your testimonies are very sure;
holiness adorns Your house,
O LORD, forever.

*I can tell time by the tides; I have seen
coastlines carved by the currents; I have been
bounced and battered by the breakers. I am in
awe of the ocean. But You are mightier than the
breakers. I stand in awe of You, Lord of the
Seas.—SB*

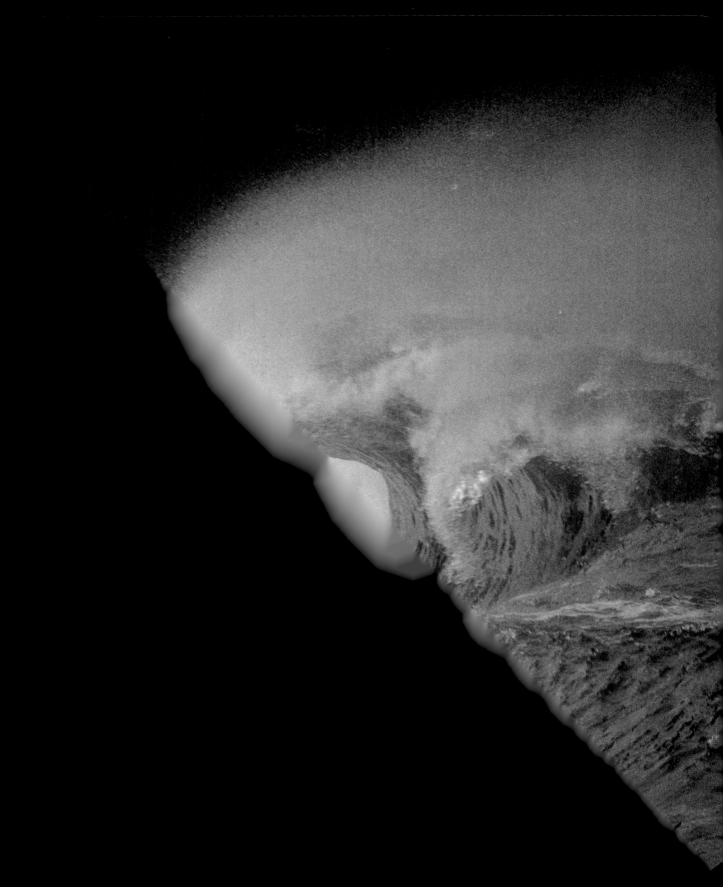

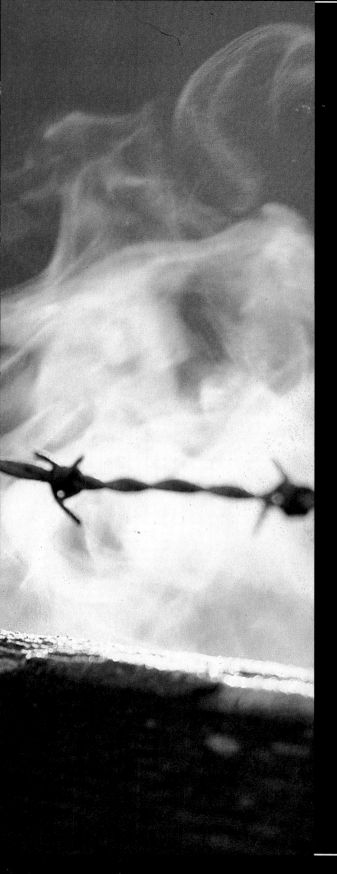

O God Who Avenges, Shine Forth

O LORD God, to whom vengeance belongs—
O God, to whom vengeance belongs, shine forth!
Rise up, O Judge of the earth;
render punishment to the proud.
LORD, how long will the wicked,
how long will the wicked triumph?
They utter speech, and speak insolent things;
all the workers of iniquity boast in themselves.
They break in pieces Your people, O LORD,
and afflict Your heritage.
They slay the widow and the stranger,
and murder the fatherless.
Yet they say, "The LORD does not see,
nor does the God of Jacob understand."
Understand, you senseless among the people;
and you fools, when will you be wise?
He who planted the ear, shall He not hear?
He who formed the eye, shall He not see?
He who instructs the nations, shall He not correct,
He who teaches man knowledge?
The LORD knows the thoughts of man,
that they are futile.
Blessed is the man whom You instruct, O LORD,
and teach out of Your law,
that You may give him rest from the days of adversity,
until the pit is dug for the wicked.
For the LORD will not cast off His people.
Nor will He forsake His inheritance.
But judgment will return to righteousness,
and all the upright in heart will follow it.

We have good reason to be ashamed, Lord. Our best endeavours may well end as a heap of glowing ashes, smoking into nothingness. Our keen minds produce logic as twisted as the wire we use to shield our pitiful prejudice and imprison that which offers us challenge. Forgive us, Lord, and cast a beam of righteous reality upon us.—SB

He Will Repay

Who will rise up for me against the evildoers?
Who will stand up for me against the
workers of iniquity?
Unless the LORD had been my help,
my soul would soon have settled in silence.
If I say, "My foot slips,"
Your mercy, O LORD, will hold me up.
In the multitude of my anxieties within me,
Your comforts delight my soul.
Shall the throne of iniquity, which devises evil by law,
have fellowship with You?
They gather together against the life of the righteous,
and condemn innocent blood.
But the LORD has been my defense,
and my God the rock of my refuge.
He has brought on them their own iniquity,
and shall cut them off in their own wickedness;
the LORD our God shall cut them off.

*Love has strong arms. Strong enough to steady
my step if I slip, to take hold of my shivering
heart and restore its steady rhythm. Love's
arms lift me up and set me high upon a rock.
From that holy vantage point wicked men look
insignificant, which, says love, they are! Love
ought to know, because love is God.—JB*

Shout Aloud to the Rock

Oh come, let us sing to the LORD!
Let us shout joyfully to the Rock of our salvation.
Let us come before His presence with thanksgiving;
let us shout joyfully to Him with psalms.
For the LORD is the great God,
and the great King above all gods.
In His hand are the deep places of the earth;
the heights of the hills are His also.
The sea is His, for He made it;
and His hands formed the dry land.
Oh come, let us worship and bow down;
let us kneel before the LORD our Maker.
For He is our God,
and we are the people of His pasture,
and the sheep of His hand.
Today, if you will hear His voice:
"Do not harden your hearts, as in the rebellion,
and as in the day of trial in the wilderness,
when your fathers tested Me; they proved Me,
though they saw My work.
For forty years I was grieved with that generation,
and said, 'It is a people who go astray
in their hearts,
and they do not know My ways.'
So I swore in My wrath,
'They shall not enter My rest.' "

God always hears my cries of praise, but do I always hear His voice of correction? Praise prevents my hardness of heart. It helps me hear His rebuke. True praise causes me to live a life of thankfulness that spills over into acts of practical love. A life like His!—JB

Worship the Lord

Oh, sing to the LORD a new song!
Sing to the LORD, all the earth.
Sing to the LORD, bless His name;
Proclaim the good news of His
salvation from day to day.
Declare His glory among the nations,
His wonders among all peoples.
For the LORD is great
and greatly to be praised;
He is to be feared above all gods.
For all the gods of the peoples are idols,
but the LORD made the heavens.
Honor and majesty are before Him;
strength and beauty are in His sanctuary.
Give to the LORD,
O kindreds of peoples,
give to the LORD glory and strength.
Give to the LORD the glory due His name;
bring an offering, and come into His courts.
Oh, worship the LORD in the beauty of holiness!
Tremble before Him, all the earth.
Say among the nations, "The LORD reigns;
the world also is firmly established,
it shall not be moved;
He shall judge the peoples righteously."
Let the heavens rejoice, and let the earth be glad;
let the sea roar, and all its fullness;
let the field be joyful, and all that is in it.
Then all the trees of the woods will
rejoice before the LORD.
For He is coming,
for He is coming to judge the earth.
He shall judge the world with righteousness.
And the peoples with His truth.

*I want to worship You, Lord, with the cool in
sunshine or storm, calmed poise of a mountain
peak. May I worship You with the reflective
grace of a still pond on a summer's day. And
when the invisible pressures of life blow, may I
sway to Your rhythm like branches on a breezy
day.—SB*

Light Is Shed

The LORD reigns; let the earth rejoice;
let the multitude of isles be glad!
Clouds and darkness surround Him;
righteousness and justice are the
foundation of His throne.
A fire goes before Him,
and burns up His enemies round about.
His lightnings light the world;
the earth sees and trembles.
The mountains melt like wax at the
presence of the LORD,
at the presence of the Lord of the whole earth.
The heavens declare His righteousness,
and all the peoples see His glory.
Let all be put to shame who serve carved images.
Who boast of idols.
Worship Him, all you gods.
Zion hears and is glad,
and the daughters of Judah rejoice
because of Your judgments, O LORD.
For You, LORD, are most high above all the earth;
You are exalted far above all gods.
You who love the LORD, hate evil!
He preserves the souls of His saints;
He delivers them out of the hand of the wicked.
Light is sown for the righteous,
and gladness for the upright in heart.
Rejoice in the LORD, you righteous,
and give thanks at the remembrance of His holy name.

*The mysteries that surround Your being, Lord,
are so profound that to our minds they are
impenetrable—You live in the clouds and in
thick darkness. But You chose to shine forth and
the revelation is to our hearts a many
splendored thing. Thank You, Lord—and please
shine on.—SB*

The heavens are Yours,
the earth also is Yours;
the world and all its fullness,
You have founded them.

He Has Remembered His Love

Oh, sing to the LORD a new song!
For He has done marvelous things;
His right hand and His holy arm
have gained Him the victory.
The LORD has made known His salvation;
His righteousness He has openly shown
in the sight of the nations.
He has remembered His mercy and His
faithfulness to the house of Israel;
all the ends of the earth have seen the
salvation of our God.
Shout joyfully to the LORD, all the earth;
break forth in song, rejoice, and sing praises.
Sing to the LORD with the harp,
with the harp and the sound of a psalm,
with trumpets and the sound of a horn;
shout joyfully before the LORD, the King.
Let the sea roar, and all its fullness,
the world and those who dwell in it;
let the rivers clap their hands;
let the hills be joyful together
before the LORD,
for He is coming to judge the earth.
With righteousness He shall judge the world,
and the peoples with equity.

The new song we are to sing is a song of judgment! Of putting things right. That seems a strange thing to sing about. Strange, that is, unless you have a child who has been molested or have lost your mate to a scheming neighbor—or have been dismissed from your job because you are a believer. Then it does not seem such strange music after all!—JB

He Loves Justice

The LORD reigns;
let the peoples tremble!
He dwells between the cherubim:
let the earth be moved!
The LORD is great in Zion.
And He is high above all the peoples.
Let them praise Your great and awesome name—
He is holy.
The King's strength also loves justice;
You have established equity;
You have executed justice and
righteousness in Jacob.
Exalt the LORD our God,
and worship at His footstool;
for He is holy.
Moses and Aaron were among His priests,
and Samuel was among those who
called upon His name;
They called upon the LORD,
and He answered them.
He spoke to them in the cloudy pillar;
they kept His testimonies and the
ordinance that He gave them.
You answered them, O LORD our God;
You were to them God-Who-Forgives,
though You took vengeance on their deeds.
Exalt the LORD our God,
and worship at His holy hill;
for the LORD our God is holy.

Lord, I need to love justice as You love it. Help me to reject the half-truth and to curb the ready exageration that leaps so easily to my lips. Teach me to honor my word as You honor Yours. Show me how to be fair with my advice. Urge my ears to judge gossip and reject it. Let it be said of me, "She loves justice!" Then You will smile.—JB

We Are His

Make a joyful shout to the LORD,
all you lands!
Serve the LORD with gladness;
come before His presence with singing.
Know that the LORD, He is God;
it is He who has made us,
and not we ourselves;
we are His people and the sheep of His pasture.
Enter into His gates with thanksgiving,
and into His courts with praise.
Be thankful to Him, and bless His name.
For the LORD is good;
His mercy is everlasting,
and His truth endures to all generations.

There is a beauty in belonging. It's the beauty of a ray of light that leads along a shadowy path, and it's the beauty of growing tall with roots in the soft warmth of fertility. Belonging to You, Lord, is that and much more: truly You are God.—SB

Join the Faithful in the Land

I will sing of mercy and justice;
to You, O LORD, I will sing praises.
I will behave wisely in a perfect way.
Oh, when will You come to me?
I will walk within my house with a
perfect heart.
I will set nothing wicked before my eyes;
I hate the work of those who fall away;
it shall not cling to me.
A perverse heart shall depart from me;
I will not know wickedness.
Whoever secretly slanders his neighbor,
him I will destroy;
the one who has a haughty look and a proud heart,
him I will not endure.
My eyes shall be on the faithful of the land,
that they may dwell with me;
he who walks in a perfect way, he shall serve me.
He who works deceit shall not dwell
within my house;
he who tells lies shall not continue in my presence.
Early I will destroy all the wicked of the land,
that I may cut off all the evildoers
from the city of the LORD.

*I can't choose my compatriots but I can choose
my companions. I don't control what people
show but I can decide what I will see, and
when slander fills the air I can stop my ears.
Give me proper desire, Lord, that I might decide
aright.*—SB

Answer Me Quickly

Hear my prayer, O LORD,
and let my cry come to You.
Do not hide Your face from me in the
day of my trouble;
incline Your ear to me; in the day that I call,
answer me speedily.
For my days are consumed like smoke,
and my bones are burned like a hearth.
My heart is stricken and withered like grass,
so that I forget to eat my bread.
Because of the sound of my groaning
my bones cling to my skin.
I am like a pelican of the wilderness;
I am like an owl of the desert.
I lie awake,
and am like a sparrow alone on the housetop.
My enemies reproach me all day long,
and those who deride me swear an oath against me.
For I have eaten ashes like bread,
and mingled my drink with weeping,
because of Your indignation and Your wrath;
for You have lifted me up and cast me away.
My days are like a shadow that lengthens,
and I wither away like grass.

Children demand immediate responses to their
wishes. Our heavenly Father understands our
childishness, yet looks for trust from us in
silent times. He asks us to mature, to grow in
silence—to wait the darkness out. We need to
use our faith to help us wait till God answers
us.—JB

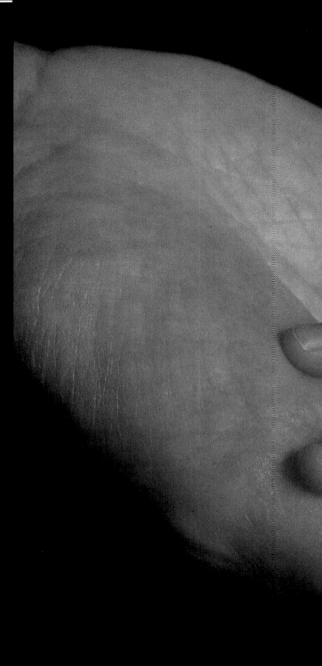

Live for a Future Generation

But You, O Lord, shall endure forever,
and the remembrance of Your name to
all generations.
You will arise and have mercy on Zion;
for the time to favor her,
yes, the set time, has come.
For Your servants take pleasure in her stones,
and show favor to her dust.
So the nations shall fear the name of the Lord,
and all the kings of the earth Your glory.
For the Lord shall build up Zion;
He shall appear in His glory.
He shall regard the prayer of the destitute,
and shall not despise their prayer.
This will be written for the geneartion to come,
that a people yet to be created may praise the Lord.
For He looked down from the height of His sanctuary;
from heaven the Lord viewed the earth,
to hear the groaning of the prisoner,
to loose those appointed to death,
to declare the name of the Lord in Zion,
and His praise in Jerusalem,
when the peoples are gathered together,
and the kingdoms, to serve the Lord.
He weakened my strength in the way;
He shortened my days.
I said, "O my God,
do not take me away in the midst of my days;
Your years are throughout all generations.
Of old You laid the foundation of the earth,
and the heavens are the work of Your hands.
They will perish, but You will endure;
yes, all of them will grow old like a garment;
like a cloak You will change them,
and they will be changed.
But You are the same,
and Your years will have no end.
The children of Your servants will continue,
and their descendants will be established before You."

There are many ways we can create a Christian heritage for our children. We can write wise words to them. We can invest money for their education. We can bequeath Bibles and godly books to them. Most of all, we can be the people God wants us to be, serving our own generation and caring for others. This sort of life writes words that will never pass away.—JB

Forget Not All His Benefits

Bless the LORD, O my soul;
and all that is within me,
bless His holy name!
Bless the LORD, O my soul,
and forget not all His benefits:
who forgives all your iniquities,
who heals all your diseases,
who redeems your life from destruction,
who crowns you with lovingkindness
and tender mercies,
who satisfies your mouth with good things,
so that your youth is renewed like the eagle's.
The LORD executes righteousness
and justice for all who are oppressed.
He made known His ways to Moses,
His acts to the children of Israel.
The LORD is merciful and gracious,
slow to anger, and abounding in mercy.
He will not always strive with us,
nor will He keep His anger forever.
He has not dealt with us according to our sins,
nor punished us according to our iniquities.
For as the heavens are high above the earth,
so great is His mercy toward those who fear Him;
as far as the east is from the west,
so far has He removed our transgressions from us.
As a father pities his children,
so the LORD pities those who fear Him.
For He knows our frame;
He remembers that we are dust.

*My memory is the thing I forget with, Lord. I
need help even to remember Your benefits.
Seeing a father with small children helps. It
reminds me of Your gentle greatness and your
forgiving firmness. Keep the reminders coming,
Lord. I must never be allowed to forget.—SB*

Because he has set his love upon Me,
therefore I will deliver him;
I will set him on high,
because he has known My name.

From Everlasting to Everlasting the Lord's Love Is

As for man, his days are like grass;
as a flower of the field, so he flourishes.
For the wind passes over it, and it is gone,
and its place remembers it no more.
But the mercy of the LORD is from
everlasting to everlasting on those who fear Him,
and His righteousness to children's children,
to such as keep His covenant,
and to those who remember His
commandments to do them.
The LORD has established His throne in heaven,
and His kingdom rules over all.
Bless the LORD, you His angels,
who excel in strength, who do His word,
heeding the voice of His word.
Bless the LORD, all you His hosts,
you ministers of His, who do His pleasure.
Bless the LORD, all His works,
in all places of His dominion.
Bless the LORD, O my soul!

I do not like to think of myself as a frail, fragile, flower, flourishing and fading away. But I must when I consider eternity. And that reminds me of the everlasting nature of Your love and the eternal dimensions of my being. Then I settle down in Your strong hands and I am satisfied. —SB

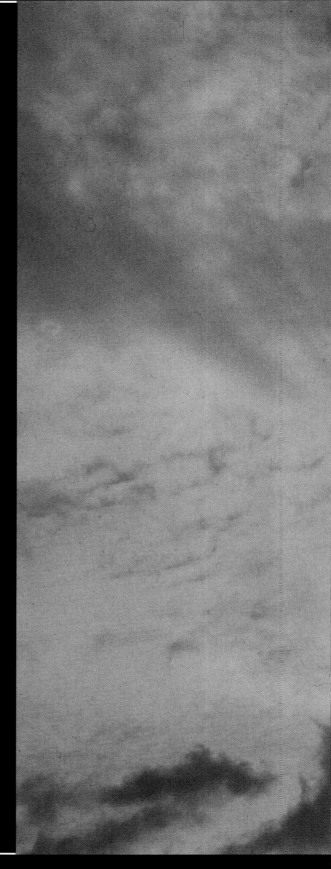

He Makes the Clouds His Chariot

Bless the LORD, O my soul!
O LORD my God, You are very great:
You are clothed with honor and majesty,
who cover Yourself with light
as with a garment,
who stretch out the heavens like a curtain.
He lays the beams of His upper chambers
in the waters,
who makes the clouds His chariot,
who walks on the wings of the wind,
who makes His angels spirits,
His ministers a flame of fire.
You who laid the foundations of the earth,
so that it should not be moved forever,
You covered it with the deep
as with a garment;
the waters stood above the mountains.
At Your rebuke they fled;
at the voice of Your thunder
they hastened away.
They went up over the mountains;
they went down into the valleys,
to the place which You founded for them.
You have set a boundary that they may not
pass over,
that they may not return to cover the earth.
He sends the springs into the valleys,
which flow among the hills.
They give drink to every beast of the field;
the wild donkeys quench their thirst.
By them the birds of the heavens have their
habitation;
they sing among the branches.

*We know God does not really ride in
a chariot made of clouds or travel on
the wings of the wind. Poetry and
imagery remind us the Lord is
Master of the winds and waves, Lord
of the birds and animals. Nature,
after all, is simply God's being
Himself—what is normal to Him is a
miracle to us.—JB*

The Earth Is Satisfied

He waters the hills from His upper chambers;
the earth is satisfied with the fruit of
Your works.
He causes the grass to grow for the cattle,
and vegetation for the service of man,
that he may bring forth food from the earth,
and wine that makes glad the heart of man,
oil to make his face shine,
and bread which strengthens man's heart.
The trees of the LORD are full of sap,
the cedars of Lebanon which He planted,
where the birds make their nests;
the stork has her home in the fir trees.
The high hills are for the wild goats;
the cliffs are a refuge for the rock badgers.
He appointed the moon for seasons;
the sun knows its going down.
You make darkness, and it is night,
in which all the beasts of the forest creep about.
The young lions roar after their prey,
and seek their food from God.
When the sun arises, they gather together
and lie down in their dens.
Man goes out to his work
and to his labor until the evening.

*God works hard working the works of creation.
Man is made in the image of God; so when man
works hard till the going down of the sun, he
mirrors that image. The Christian should have a
healthy sense of the rightness of work. He
should know that doing a good job with the
right attitude is telling people what God is
like.—JB*

May the Lord Rejoice in His Works

O LORD, how manifold are Your works!
In wisdom You have made them all.
The earth is full of Your possessions—
this great and wide sea,
in which are innumerable teeming things,
living things both small and great.
There the ships sail about;
and there is that Leviathan
which You have made to play there.
These all wait for You,
that You may give them their food in due
season.
What You give them they gather in;
You open Your hand, they are filled with
good.
You hide Your face, they are troubled;
You take away their breath,
they die and return to their dust.
You send forth Your Spirit, they are created;
And You renew the face of the earth.
May the glory of the LORD endure forever;
may the LORD rejoice in His works.
He looks on the earth, and it trembles;
He touches the hills, and they smoke.
I will sing to the LORD as long as I live;
I will sing praise to my God while I have
my being.
May my meditation be sweet to Him;
I will be glad in the LORD.
May sinners be consumed from the earth,
and the wicked be no more.
Bless the LORD, O my soul!
Praise the LORD!

*I love to think of Your rejoicing,
Lord. Sitting in glory and delighting
in the seas shimmering silver in the
sunlight and the tall ships buoyed by
the depths and blown by the breeze.
But You made me, too; I would like
to be a cause for rejoicing as
well.*—SB

Tell of All His Wonderful Acts

Oh, give thanks to the LORD!
Call upon His name....
Remember His marvelous works which He has done,
His wonders, and the judgments of His mouth,
O seed of Abraham His servant,
you children of Jacob, His chosen ones!
He is the LORD our God;
His judgments are in all the earth.
He has remembered His covenant forever,
the word which He commanded,
for a thousand generations,
the covenant which He made with Abraham,
and His oath to Isaac,
and confirmed it to Jacob for a statute,
to Israel for an everlasting covenant,
saying, "To you I will give the land of Canaan
as the allotment of your inheritance,"
when they were but few in number,
indeed very few, and strangers in it.
When they went from one nation to another,
from one kingdom to another people,
He permitted no one to do them wrong;
yes, He reproved kings for their sakes,
saying, "Do not touch My anointed ones,
and do My prophets no harm."
Moreover He called for a famine in the land;
He destroyed all the provision of bread.
He sent a man before them—
Joseph—who was sold as a slave.
They hurt his feet with fetters,
he was laid in irons.
Until the time that his word came to pass,
the word of the LORD tested him.
The king sent and released him,
the ruler of the people let him go free.
He made him lord of his house,
and ruler of all his possessions,
to bind his princes at his pleasure,
and teach his elders wisdom.

*It takes many flowers to make a garden, many
stones to build a belfry, many trees to grow a
forest. And it takes lots of persons to make a
people. How precious is each person—how
crucial for his people. As was Joseph, whom
You used to do wonderful things for his people
and for our world.—SB*

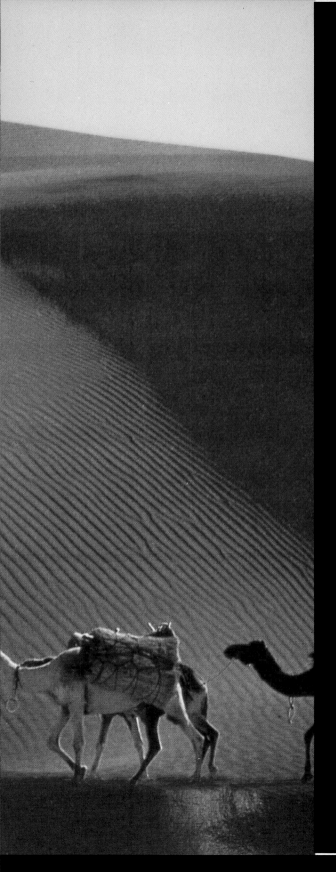

Then Israel Entered Egypt

Israel also came into Egypt,
and Jacob sojourned in the land of Ham.
And He increased His people greatly,
and made them stronger than their enemies.
He turned their heart to hate His people,
to deal craftily with His servants.
He sent Moses His servant,
and Aaron whom He had chosen.
They performed His signs among them,
and wonders in the land of Ham.
He sent darkness, and made it dark;
and they did not rebel against His word.
He turned their waters into blood,
and killed their fish.
Their land abounded with frogs,
even in the chambers of their kings.
He spoke, and there came swarms of flies,
and lice in all their territory.
He gave them hail for rain,
and flaming fire in their land.
He struck their vines also,
and their fig trees,
and splintered the trees of their territory.
He spoke, and locusts came,
young locusts without number,
and ate up all the vegetation in their land,
and devoured the fruit of their ground.
He also destroyed all the firstborn in their land,
the first of all their strength.

A diamond sparkles when it is set against black velvet. When Israel entered Egypt, God placed His precious jewel against the shadows of the plagues and displayed His most precious gem. When you find yourself in Egypt, be still and let God display Himself through you. That way He will bring great glory to Himself.—JB

He Remembered His Holy Promise

He also brought them out with
silver and gold,
and there was none feeble
among His tribes.
Egypt was glad when they departed,
for the fear of them had fallen upon them.
He spread a cloud for a covering,
and fire to give light in the night.
The people asked, and He brought quail,
and satisfied them with the bread of
heaven.
He opened the rock, and water gushed out;
it ran in the dry places like a river.
For He remembered His holy promise,
and Abraham His servant.
He brought out His people with joy,
His chosen ones with gladness.
He gave them the lands of the Gentiles,
and they inherited the labor of the nations,
that they might observe His statutes
and keep His laws.
Praise the LORD!

*How many of us have fallen heir to
what others have toiled for? God
blesses us that we may be a
blessing. We are saved to serve. God
is on our side that we may use our
prosperity on behalf of the poor. Our
spiritual heritage should be used to
bring light to those who sit in
darkness.*—JB

Bless the Lord, O my soul;
and all that is within me,
bless His holy name!
Bless the Lord, O my soul,
and forget not all his benefits.

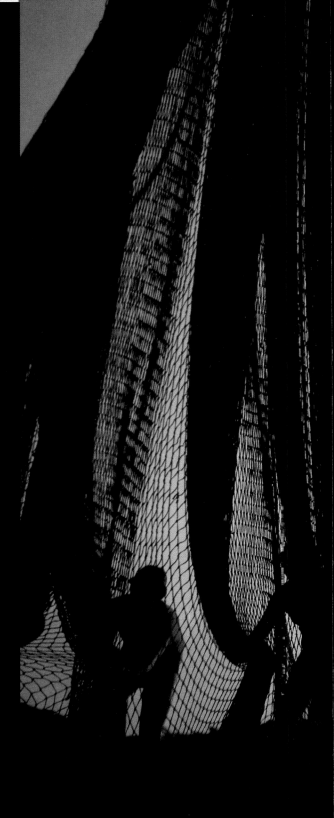

He Saved Them
for His Name's Sake

Praise the LORD!
Oh, give thanks to the LORD, for He is good!
For His mercy endures forever.
Who can utter the mighty acts of the LORD?
Blessed are those who keep justice,
and he who does righteousness at all times!
Remember me, O LORD, with the favor
You have toward Your people;
oh, visit me with Your salvation,
that I may see the benefit of Your chosen ones,
that I may rejoice in the gladness of Your nation,
that I may glory with Your inheritance.
We have sinned with our fathers,
we have committed iniquity, we have done wickedly.
Our fathers in Egypt did not understand Your wonders;
they did not remember the multitude of Your mercies,
but rebelled by the sea—the Red Sea.
Nevertheless He saved them for His name's sake,
that He might make His mighty power known.
He rebuked the Red Sea also, and it dried up;
so He led them through the depths,
as through the wilderness.
The waters covered their enemies;
there was not one of them left.
Then they believed His words; they sang His praise.
They soon forgot His works;
they did not wait for His counsel,
but lusted exceedingly in the wilderness,
and tested God in the desert.
And He gave them their request,
but sent leanness into their soul.
When they envied Moses in the camp,
and Aaron the saint of the LORD,
the earth opened up and swallowed Dathan,
and covered the faction of Abiram.
A fire was kindled in their company;
the flame burned up the wicked.

*We, Your people, can become like the dry,
parched ground—hard and callous in our
disobedience. But You send the showers only to
see them soak into the ruts of indifference. Save
us, Lord, and fill us till the pools of blessing
reflect your glory and till all people say
"Amen."—JB*

They Despised
the Pleasant Land

They made a calf in Horeb,
and worshiped the molded image.
Thus they changed their glory
into the image of an ox that eats grass.
They forgot God their Savior,
who had done great things in Egypt,
wondrous works in the land of Ham,
awesome things by the Red Sea.
Therefore He said that He would destroy them,
had not Moses His chosen one stood before Him
in the breach,
to turn away His wrath, lest He destroy them.
Then they despised the pleasant land;
they did not believe His word,
but murmured in their tents,
and did not heed the voice of the LORD.
Therefore He lifted up His hand in an oath
against them,
to overthrow them in the wilderness,
to overthrow their descendants among the nations,
and to scatter them in the lands.
They joined themselves also to Baal of Peor,
and ate sacrifices made to the dead.
Thus they provoked Him to anger with their deeds,
and the plague broke out among them.
Then Phinehas stood up and intervened,
and so the plague was stopped.
And that was accounted to him for righteousness to all
generations forevermore.
They angered Him also at the waters of strife,
so that it went ill with Moses on account of them;
because they rebelled against His Spirit,
so that he spoke rashly with his lips.

*The most pleasant land can be hidden in the
deepest gloom. The most precious promises can
lie buried under the rubble of unseemly
attitudes and unspeakable attitudes. I know,
Lord, for I have been in such a place. Banish
the clouds, break up the rubble and show me
the pastures full of life.—SB*

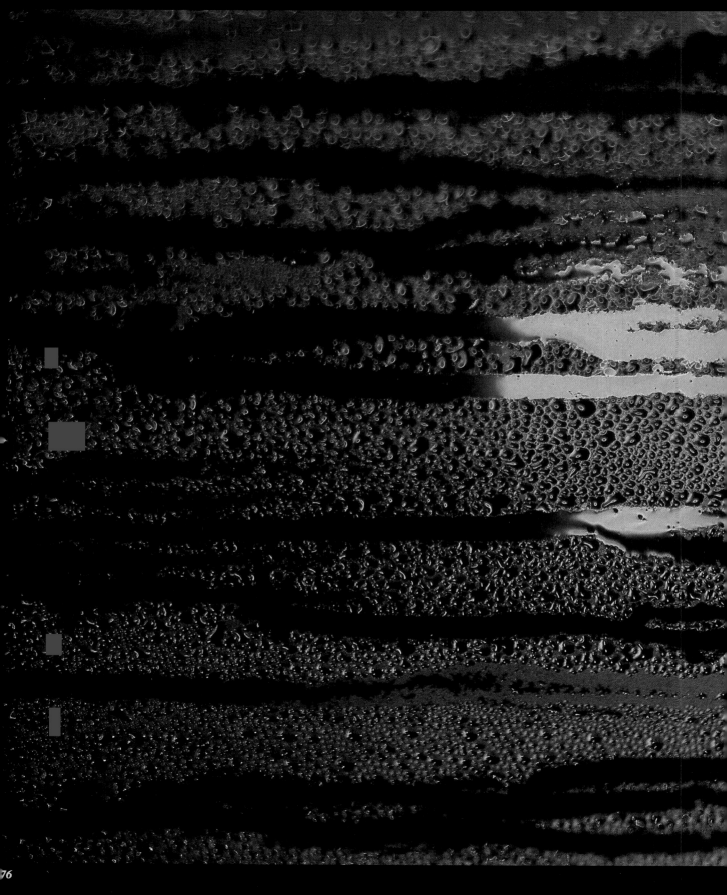

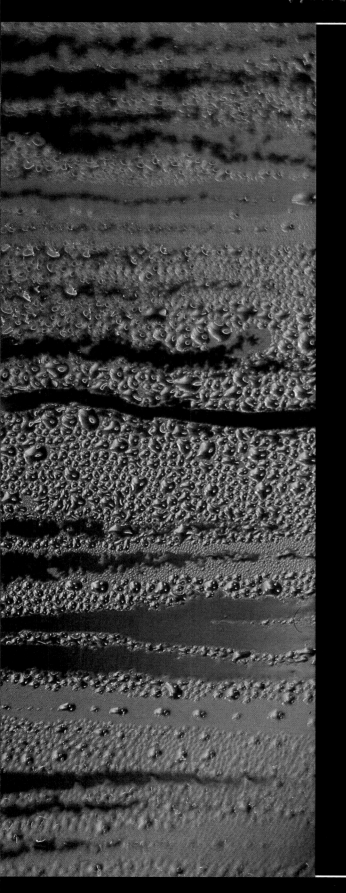

Let All the People Say, "Amen!"

They did not destroy the peoples,
concerning whom the LORD had commanded them,
but they mingled with the Gentiles
and learned their works;
they served their idols,
which became a snare to them.
They even sacrificed their sons
and their daughters to demons,
and shed innocent blood,
even the blood of their sons and daughters,
whom they sacrificed to the idols of Canaan;
and the land was polluted with blood.
Thus they were defiled by their own works,
and played the harlot by their own deeds.
Therefore the wrath of the LORD was
kindled against His people,
so that He abhorred His own inheritance.
And He gave them into the hand of the Gentiles,
and those who hated them ruled over them.
Their enemies also oppressed them,
and they were brought into subjection
under their hand.
Many times He delivered them;
but they rebelled against Him by their counsel,
and were brought low for their iniquity.
Nevertheless He regarded their affliction,
when He heard their cry;
and for their sake He remembered His covenant,
and relented according to the multitude of His mercies.
He also made them to be pitied
by all those who carried them away captive.
Save us, O LORD our God,
and gather us from among the Gentiles,
to give thanks to Your holy name,
and to triumph in Your praise.
Blessed be the LORD God of Israel
from everlasting to everlasting!
And let all the people say, "Amen!"
Praise the LORD!

*God takes His promises very seriously, even
when we forget the things we have promised
Him. He loves and chastens us, as a father
corrects his children. He works on our behalf
even when we would rather be left alone. He
insists on being faithful—I'm glad!—JB*

77

For as the heavens are high above the earth, so great is His mercy toward those who fear Him. As far as the east is from the west, so far has he removed our transgressions from us.

*Blessed be the God of Israel
from everlasting to everlasting!
And let all the people*